My Country
China

Jillian Powell

A+

Smart Apple Media

Published by Smart Apple Media
P.O. Box 3263, Mankato, Minnesota 56002
www.blackrabbitbooks.com

Published by arrangement with the Watts Publishing Group
LTD, London.

Library of Congress Cataloging-in-Publication Data
Powell, Jillian. China / Jillian Powell.
p. cm. — (My country)
Summary: "Readers are introduced to Li, who describes
China's people, festivals, landscape, and food. Includes a
fact page on China's population, geography, and culture"
—Provided by publisher.
Includes bibliographical references and index.
ISBN 978-1-59920-903-6 (library binding)
1. China—Juvenile literature. I. Title.
DS706.P68 2015
951—dc23
          2012024745

Series Editor: Paul Rockett
Series Designer: Paul Cherrill for Basement68
Picture Researcher: Diana Morris

Every attempt has been made to clear copyright. Should
there be any inadvertent omission please apply to the
publisher for rectification.

Picture credits: Atlaspix/Shutterstock: 4b; Chrispyphoto/
Dreamstime: 13t, 15t; ekier/Shutterstock: 22b; fototrav/
istockphoto: 5; Willaume Gautier/Shutterstock: 7t; grafica/
Shutterstock: front cover c, 4t, 7b, 13b, 15b, 19b, 21 inset,
22t; Cyril Hou/Shutterstock: 12; Hupeng/Dreamstime:
17; Catherine Karnow/Corbis: 14, 24; James Lee 999/
istockphoto: 3, 9; Logit/Dreamstime: 6; Fen Osbourne/
Photogenes: 20; Daniel Prudek/Shutterstock: 8; Cora
Reed/Shutterstock: front cover l; Viewstock/Alamy:
18; Vincent369/Shutterstock: front cover r; Ke Wang/
Shutterstock: 2, 21; Windmoon/Shutterstock: 19t; Fei
Xie/Dreamstime: 11; Ron Yue/Alamy: 10; Zyon-Lebleavec/
sagaphoto.com/Alamy: 1, 16.

Printed in Stevens Point, Wisconsin at Worzalla
PO 1654
4-2014

9 8 7 6 5 4 3 2 1

Contents

All words in **bold** appear in the glossary on page 23.

China in the World

My name is Li and I live in China.

This is the **Chinese character** for my name: 力

In China, we use characters instead of an alphabet.

Beijing

Shanghai

Hong Kong

china's place in the world

China is the fourth largest country in the world and the largest within Asia. It shares borders with 14 other countries.

I live in Beijing. It is a big, busy city with tall skyscrapers and lots of amazing things to see.

People Who Live in China

More people live in China than any other country in the world. Most of us speak Mandarin Chinese but many other languages are spoken in different **regions**.

In the cities, people work in banks, shops, offices, and factories.

Here are people working on a rice plantation in the country.

People live in cities or in small towns or villages in the country where they grow crops or herd sheep or goats.

We make clothes, toys, games, and many other things that are sold all over the world.

China's Landscape

China is so big it has many different types of landscapes, from tall mountains and highlands to wide **deserts** and flat plains.

There are rivers and waterfalls, thick forests, and rocky landforms of towers and caves.

Two-humped camels live in the Gobi Desert.

These people, dressed in traditional clothes, are picking tea leaves.

China has a long coastline and many islands. To the southwest are the Himalayan Mountains.

Crops such as tea grow on **terraces** cut into steep hillsides.

At Home with My Family

In China, most families who live in a city have only one child. I live with my mom, my dad, and my grandma.

We live in an apartment that has three bedrooms, a bathroom, and a cooking and dining area. There is also a small balcony.

This is our block of apartments. We live on the ninth floor, so we can see over the city.

On weekends, we often go to the park together. Lots of people go there to have fun and exercise.

Sometimes Dad takes me go-karting with my friends. I also like shopping at the market with Grandma.

Street markets sell clothes and crafts, as well as food.

My favorite pastimes are go-karting and ping-pong. What are yours?

What We Eat

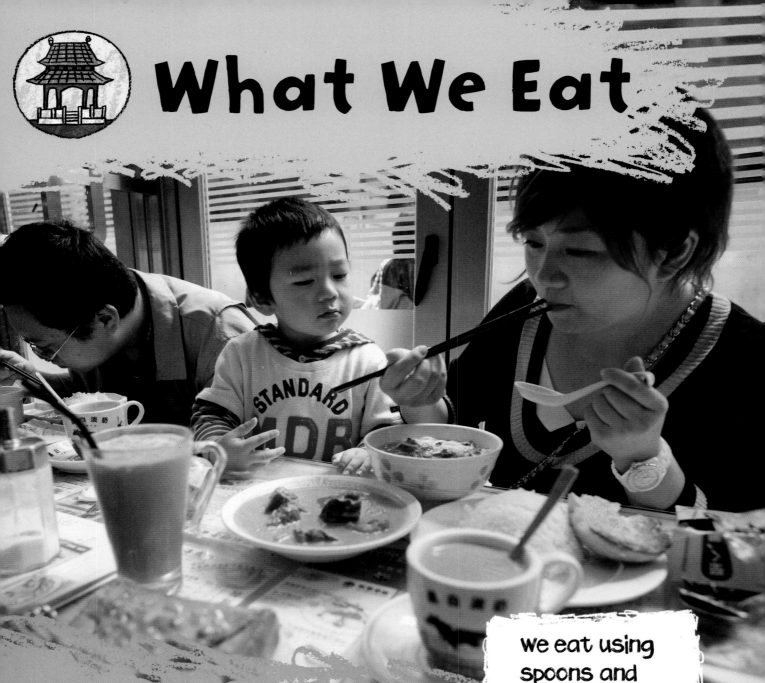

we eat using spoons and chopsticks.

For breakfast, we have rice or noodles and drink tea. I have a hot lunch at school.

For dinner, we share dishes of meat, fish or **tofu**, rice, and vegetables.

This is a kebab stall. Kebabs are made of meat, seafood, and sometimes bugs, such as scorpions!

Kebabs and dim sum, which are little steamed dumplings or rolls with tasty fillings, are also popular in China.

They are eaten with tea in restaurants and sold by street sellers as fast food snacks.

My favorite food is dim sum!

15

Going to School

Most children start school when they are six years old.

Every morning we sing our **national anthem** and raise the Chinese flag.

We have lessons in Chinese language and literature, math, and moral education, which teaches us how to behave well toward others.

We salute the flag during the morning flag-raising ceremony.

At our morning break, we do our exercises, which include lots of stretching.

At lunchtime, we listen to a story or we do some homework.

In the afternoons, we usually do sports or arts and crafts.

Art lessons are fun! My favorite color is red, which is a lucky color in China.

Festivals and Celebrations

We have lots of colorful festivals with fireworks and street parades.

Chinese New Year begins with the first new moon of the year. On the 15th day, there is a Lantern Festival.

For the Lantern Festival, children parade through the streets carrying lanterns.

In spring, there is a Dragon Boat Festival. People race boats and eat special rice dumplings.

For children in China, our sixth birthday is an important one. Families get together and eat long noodles to bring us luck and a long life.

In dragon boat racing, the boat is decorated with a dragon's head.

I like Chinese New Year. Children are given red envelopes of money.

 # Things to See

Many people come to see the Great Wall of China, which is over 2,000 years old and stretches 5,500 miles (8,800 km). It crosses mountains, deserts, and plains. I can see part of the wall from Beijing.

The Great Wall of china is the worlds longest wall.

Tourists like to see China's beautiful **pagodas**, and the famous **terracotta** soldiers and horses. This army was made for the **tomb** of the First Emperor of China.

The Terracotta Army has over 8,000 soldiers and 600 horses, all life-size.

I want to go to see the giant pandas at the Chengdu Panda Base.

> Here are some facts about my country!

Fast Facts about China

Capital city = Beijing
Population = 1.35 billion
Currency = the yuan
Area = 3,706,580 square miles
  (9.6 million km²)
Main language = Mandarin Chinese
National holiday = Chinese New Year
Main religions = Buddhism, Islam,
  Christianity, Taoism
Longest river = Yangtze River, 3,915 miles (6,300 km)
Highest mountain = Mount Everest, 29,029 feet (8,848 m)

Glossary

Chinese character a word written in the Chinese language

deserts dry lands which have little or no rain

monsoon heavy seasonal rains

national anthem a song of praise and love for a country

pagodas temples, often built as pyramids or towers

regions parts or areas of a country

terraces flat areas, sometimes forming several levels

terracotta a type of red clay

tofu a soft, cheese-like food made from soy bean milk

tomb building that marks a grave

Further Information

Websites

www.enchantedlearning.com/asia/china

http://www.historyforkids.org/learn/china/

http://www.timeforkids.com/destination/china

Books

Crean, Susan. *Discover China (Discover Countries).*
    PowerKids Press, 2012

Savery, Annabel. *China (Been There).* Smart Apple Media, 2012

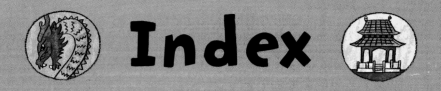

Index